I Believe
in
Miracles

Diza Sutton

I Believe in *Miracles*

Copyright © 2023 Diza Sutton
First Edition

Newman Springs Publishing
320 Broad Street
Red Bank, NJ 07701

First originally published by Newman Springs Publishing 2023

ISBN 979-8-9851093-0-6 (Paperback)
ISBN 979-8-9851093-1-3 (eBook)

Printed in the United States of America

I dedicate this story to my Lord and Savior; for without Him, there would be no miracles. Amen!

Contents

. . . .

Acknowledgments

. . . .

To my children, I loved you with all that I am, from the day you were born. To my seven grandchildren and four great-grandchildren, I thank God for blessing me to be a part of your lives. I'm proud of each one of you, I love you. I will forever be your Nana, your Grandma Dottie. Hallelujah! Tina and Bre, I want you to know, you are forever in my heart. I love you.

To my oldest brother, John (we call him Bug or Johnnie). Even though you did not live to read my story, I know you are looking down on me and saying, "Well done." You played a major role in my life. I am forever grateful to be your sister. I love you. You are missed *SO,-SO dearly*.

To my best friend in the whole world since fourth grade, I loved you for who you are. Friends for life. I love your smile, Doris.

To my bro Jimmy, you will always hold a special place in my heart. No matter what, I will always—and I do mean always—love you.

To Sylvia, my friend, to the end, I love you. You were there for me when no one else was. I am forever blessed to have you as a true friend. Thank you.

Betty, you were the first lady I met when I moved to Virginia, and we remain friends. Thank you for being there for me. I love your smile.

I saved the best for last. To my beloved Bishop Bell and First Lady Mrs. Bell, you have always been there for me. I remember walking over twenty years ago to that small building. God led me to what I felt was home and you were my family. I want you to know that I love you both from the core of my heart.

Mrs. Wells, you made it possible for me to share my story from the beginning.

Thank you Jesus, I love you, Lord.

May God, bless you, all.

Introduction

· ·

As I sit here in this lonely jail cell with nothing to do, it dawned on me to write in my little diary. This diary will help me remember what happens while I am here and what has happened to bring me to this point. My mind wants so badly to forget and never look back again, but I must keep it fresh in my mind (at least, until my court date). Even then, I do not know if I can put this behind me.

It all started on Friday, October 14, 1994. As always, I got Niva, my daughter, dressed for school; then I walked her to the bus stop at Twentieth and Chicago Avenue. I came back home because I had some overnight out-of-town guests. When I returned home, my guests told me they were heading home. After saying my goodbyes, I went over to my friend Sylveta's house. Sylveta was a neighbor who lived across the street from me. I was always at her house, or she hung out at mine.

That morning, we stayed in the den, drinking and listening to oldies but goodies. The small get-together at Sylveta's consisted of me, Patrick, and Sylveta. We talked, laughed, cracked jokes, smoked, and drank. We drank about two twelve-packs of Budweiser beer and Colt 45. I later went back to my house to get something and saw that my guests were still there. Suddenly, Ben came down the stairs and spoke to me.

He said, "Hi, Dee. What's up?" I replied, "Nothing much," and then I introduced him to my guests. Ben started telling me that he cooked a nice steak dinner for Moe (that is what he called my oldest daughter, Monica). I told him not to tell me about a steak dinner since he did not bring me any. We all started laughing. I then told him and my guests, who were leaving at that time, that I was going back to Sylveta's house. I said my goodbyes to them for a final time, and they got into the car and drove off. I left Ben at my house and went back to Sylveta's to listen to more "oldies but goodies" music and to continue drinking beer. Later, I went back home.

It was time for my daughter Niva to come home from school. When she came in, I told her that Ben was upstairs. She ran upstairs to where he was. Wallace, my ex, came to my home early that day as we were going to cash his check. I told Niva that I was going out and asked if she wanted to come. She told me no because she and Ben were playing Nintendo. So, Wallace and I went to cash his check and came back. Shortly after, I started frying fish. When I finished, I yelled upstairs for them to come down to eat. Ben never came downstairs, so the three of us blessed our food and sat down to eat.

After some time, I decided to go upstairs for the first time all day. It is not unusual for me because I don't like stairs. When I wake up in the mornings and go downstairs, I stay there and do my chores and the things that need to be done. Once I have completed all the tasks downstairs, I usually go back up and stay there for the remainder of the evening. I normally watch the news. I always try to watch the evening news, especially if I miss the news at noon. But the TV I had downstairs did not work. I was ready to go upstairs.

When I went upstairs, the television was already on, and the news was showing someone that resembled Ben. For a moment, I just stared at the television because I was not sure if it was him. I thought my eyes were playing tricks on me. I then realized that my TV was on mute, so I began to search for the remote. I admit that I did not keep a neat bedroom, so I could not find the remote.

I went into my daughter's bedroom and asked Ben if he was in some kind of trouble, because his picture or someone resembling him was on the news. I did not hear what the newscasters were saying, but I asked him what was up. He only responded that he had to "get out of here." At that point, I thought it was something pertaining to drugs. I heard he was a drug dealer. I told him that he was right and that he did have to leave.

We started down the stairs. Ben went out the door, and that was the last time I saw him alive. I went back upstairs to drink a beer and get my thoughts together. I was trying to figure out what he did. I found the remote, unmuted the TV, and looked through all the channels to try and find out what was going on. After about twenty or thirty minutes, the news flash came on the television again. It said that Ben had killed some people. I was shocked and could not believe what I was hearing because he was just in my house, and I did not know a thing. He acted as if nothing ever happened. I was shocked at how or if he could do something like that.

A short while later, I was sitting on my bed, by the window. I heard someone say, "Get Down! I mean it!" There was a lot of cussing going on. I looked out the window as far as I could, and I saw a man with a flashlight. I heard a boy say, "The person you have on the ground is not the person you are looking for. You are looking for the person next door." The boy was pointing at my apartment. I told Wallace that the police were outside and that I was going to open the door.

I went downstairs and opened the front door for the police. They came in, and one officer said, "I am Detective Wilabe. Do you know why we are here?"

I said, "I guess you're looking for Ben."

He said, "Is he here?"

I said, "No."

He asked, "Has he been to your house? I have a reliable source that said he was seen in your apartment."

I said, "Yes."

The detective began questioning me about the time he was there and what he was wearing and whom he left with and so forth.

After they looked around my house, they left. Detective Wilabe warned us that we could get in big trouble for withholding information or hiding Ben. It is strange because I cooperated with them fully. I gave them all the information that I knew. I had not seen or heard from my daughter or Ben until November 17, when he was caught in New York.

During the time that Ben and my daughter were still at large, I put out a missing person's report on her. At that time, I felt that he was with her and that she did not go willingly—or that she too was dead. All I know is that I was afraid for her life, and all I could say was, "Lord, please don't let anything happen to her."

The FBI came to my house several times, asking me the same questions. The detectives also came with the media and the housing authority. The housing authority told me that I would have to move from the housing project where I lived.

I was under a lot of stress, and soon, I could not take it anymore. I went to my doctor and asked him to give me something for my nerves. I do not like taking medicine or pills. Part of the reason

I waited so long to even go to the doctor was because I was drinking every day.

My telephone lines were tapped. The FBI denied it, but I knew and could tell because they went behind my back to other people's homes to question them about me. The people they questioned would tell me that they had been questioned. They even tried to say that Ben bought me the big-screen television that I had in my living room. I told them that the television was purchased for fifty bucks and did not even work. My life was a living hell.

Ben never gave me anything. I never liked him. We had an argument the first time I met him. There was something about his eyes that was not right. My daughter was a hardworking girl. She held a job ever since she was fourteen. She was very independent and even had her own apartment at a very young age. I figured that Ben was not her type. My daughter kept her distance from me because she did not want another argument to start between me and Ben.

I was living in the JW section of Richmond when my daughter met Ben. I transferred to another low-income housing project on the Southside. My daughter purchased a car then. She had saved up her money to buy it, but the police were saying that it was Ben's car. I only tolerated Ben because of my daughter. It appears she really cared for him, and he appeared to care for her. So, I accepted the fact that they were going to be together. My daughter was my friend, and it was most devastating to me when she went missing. I no longer heard from her.

In the past, my relationship with my daughter was strange because we were not close. But we started getting our lives together, and we were beginning to become a real mother-and-daughter duo. Though we were becoming close, she still would never tell me about her personal life, and I never asked. We did not share with one another, which was a major mistake for me. She never trusted me enough to tell me what was going on in her life. I would never do anything intentionally to hurt her.

As time went on, my house continued to be under twenty-four-hour surveillance. My phones were tapped, and I was followed everywhere I went. I never tried to leave or hide anything. I told them everything. That was more than what they did for me. During this time, I was given fourteen charges. I lost everything but my faith, and still, I felt like a lost soul.

I must admit I do feel sorry and very sad for the family and children who were killed by Ben, and for the hurt that the family members left behind had to deal with. We could have been victims too. Well, in a sense, we were because what Ben did affect my family—and forever will. Ben didn't appear, to me and to others, to be capable of committing such a heinous crime.

The thing that gets to me the most is that all children loved him, and he appeared to love them. I had my daughter Niva in the house, and she had just turned eleven years old. It hurts my heart to know that Ben killed children around the same age as Niva. My heart will always be broken because of what has happened to that family. If I had known where Ben was, I would have gotten that thousand-dollar reward from the beginning. Still, this tragedy has given me strength—strength in knowing that only God in Heaven above saved me. I know the good Lord will make a way out of no way. I trust and believe in Him. He is all I have.

I have been in isolation in this jail now for twenty-five days. I am in a small cell with an iron bed, a thin mattress, and a toilet with a sink attached. The food is something I would not feed anyone. In here—jail—you do not get a proper meal; instead, you get a whole lot of strange stuff that can hurt you in the end. They feed you nine slices of bread per day, along with rice, potatoes, and beans. It's enough to make you diabetic, which I am. For breakfast, all you eat are eggs, eggs, eggs, boiled, scrambled …you name it. Mostly I think they used powdered eggs.

It is so cold in this cell that sometimes I want to cry. But I have run out of tears. You can only come out of your cell twice a day: once for a shower and once to use the phone. The rest of your time is spent in this tiny, cold cell. My buttocks are so sore from lying down so much. You have just enough room to jump in place or do jumping jacks. I have been doing them.

I could not go into the population here, which is the main housing of all the inmates. They say it is for my own protection. The head personnel said that it was not a wise decision because my life may be in danger. *My life is in danger?* My life is in danger of somebody else's wrongdoing. If it were my own wrongdoing that caused me to be in here, then that would be a different issue. But I am here because of one person who had to take other people's lives, including children and babies. I feel so helpless.

I have not even been to trial yet, but the newspapers and news media have already convicted me and painted such a bad picture of me. They are adding other information to make it worse for me. I am mad! I have good reason to be. They have all pronounced me guilty. Here I am with fourteen charges. I am not even forty years old, and I am in prison. But I will tell you one thing: I will never forget my fortieth birthday. All hell broke loose that month.

December 11, 1994

Just when I thought nothing else could happen, *bam!* A bomb hit. My lawyer came to see me and told me that the district attorney told him that they have a witness who is going to testify against me. The witness said I liked Ben and that I hid him and Monica. They said I helped them escape. The witness stated that I drove them to New York. I don't have a license, and I don't even know how to drive. I am doing a whole lot of praying every day. I am asking the Lord to set me free from this bondage.

Please, Lord, have mercy on me. I have no one else to turn to. You are a merciful God. I know you will set me free. Lord, I'm so tired—tired of being locked up like a wild animal. Please help me! Lord, take away the pain. Don't let the pain ache any longer.

These are the coldest days of my life.

December 13, 1994

It is cold outside. I can tell because it is cold in this cell. The inmates are wearing sweatshirts and jackets. When I asked for one, I was told the jail did not have a size 16 sweatshirt or jacket that would fit me, but that is okay. I will make it somehow.

A Christmas song just came on. Christmas is so sad this year. I am crying every time I hear Christmas carols. I miss my daughters, Wallace, and my best friend Sylveta. I wish I could be there with them. My only hope is to wait and see if Ben is extradited here from New York. Then I can go back to the bond hearing and pray they let me out on my own recognizance or reduce my bond. If that happens, then Wallace can afford to pay to get me out. I am praying for miracles. The Lord will make a way. I know He will.

I have been taking medicine ever since all of this happened. Since being in here, the doctor has given me Diazepam, Benadryl, and Prozac. They were prescribed for my stress. They relax me and help me to sleep. I could not survive in here without them.

Today is not one of my good days. I am feeling depressed. Wallace and Niva are coming to see me. I hope it will make me feel better. I cannot take seeing them leave, and I am still here. It hurts not being able to go home with my family.

My favorite song is Nancy Wilson's "I Can't Make You Love Me"! Every time I hear that song, I cry my heart out. It is so true. I got a whole lot of mail yesterday from Boo, Wallace, and Sylveta. I was so delighted to get so much mail. It really made my night. I slept very well with my Bible. I would hold my Bible in my arms every night and pray.

A couple of females are trying to hit on me in here. I stay to myself and don't mess with anybody. One of them came up to me and started feeling my hair. They keep trying to give me things, even now as I am writing. She is lying in the next cell beside mine. She is a trustee. That is not my style. These deputies in here have something going on with these female inmates. I see, hear, and learn a lot of stuff in this hellhole.

December 19, 1994

It has been a while since I wrote in my little diary. There is not much more to tell, except that Ben went to court in New York to see if he is going to get extradited here to Virginia. It would not be until January 20, 1995, before he will go back to court. They said he would have another week to respond after that. Why does he have to respond? What is the reason? Why doesn't he feel that he should come back to Virginia? My life depends on his move. It is like playing chess—only, these are real people and real lives at stake.

My lawyer is still talking about the same old stuff. They are waiting to get him down here before we can take it back to court, to see if the judge would drop my bond down some more or let me out on my own recognizance. It is a shame. I must sit in isolation all this time. No one on the outside cares. No one is trying to get me out. My hands are tied, and I cannot do anything.

I am looking up. As days go by, I am praying, asking, begging, and pleading with the Lord to set me free from this bondage. I am keeping the faith, and I am not giving up. My daughter Niva is going through a whole lot. She needs me out just as much as I want to get out. It is so hard on her. She should not have to suffer for this no-good boy. I feel hurt, used, abused, and taken for granted by him.

Why, Lord? Why has he ruined my life like this? I don't know how much more I can bear. I am writing in my Bible, "Lord, you gave me more than I can bear."

There are six days before Christmas, and only God knows when I am going to get through this. I will, somehow, with the Lord on my side. I shall get through all of this. It has now been thirty-two days in isolation, without television or much else. I can only take a shower at 5:00 a.m. and use the telephone once a day.

My body is sore from lying down so much. There is nothing to do but read, write, sleep, and eat. You do not even go out of your cell to eat. You eat, sleep, and go to the bathroom—all in the same cell. It is worse than living in your own filth. I am so tired of looking at these bars, these walls, this toilet, and this hard iron bed. My back hurts so much. I have asked twice to go into the population and have been turned down both times.

Today, I am writing two letters to the captain: one asking him if I can go into the population and the other asking him why my uniform color is orange, for the second time. If I am charged with fourteen misdemeanors, misdemeanors wear yellow. Orange is for felonies. I am being falsely represented; don't you agree? The only response they give is "I do not know." The supervisor is not even sure what I am being charged with, which is why I am in orange. If I know, the newspapers know, the courts know, and the whole United States knows, then why is it that the jail does not know?

Since this mess started, everyone has treated me unfairly. They assume anything they want. I do not have any say, and no one hears me. It is like I do not even exist. My voice is not heard. I am being kept in this cell until the system needs me or lets me go, like some sort of prize catch. And it's Christmas.

It seems everyone has turned away from me, but that is okay. I have the Lord with me, and with Him, I shall be free. This has been His plan for me since the day I was conceived—that I will be free.

My Childhood

· ·

My name is Diza. I was born on October 5, 1954, and raised in Washington DC. My real nickname is Dottie. I changed it to Dee when I got older. I want to share a story with you that you will never forget. While I was growing up, our home was a mixture of my step-father, three stepbrothers, three whole brothers, and my stepsister.

In my early, early years (I can't remember how old I was, but I do know that it had to be my real father and not my stepfather), I remember my dad and mom fighting a lot. My nerves were a wreck. I used to run and hide under the bed and yell at the top of my lungs until they would stop fighting. Both would get down on their knees and look under the bed, saying, "Dottie, come out from under the bed. We are not fighting anymore."

Sometimes it would work, and I find myself crawling out from under the bed; but most of the time, I would just stay there. I would stay under that bed, where I felt safe and secure, sniffling the whole time. Not until I felt safe, I would come out.

I used to be a tomboy. It was no surprise as I had three whole brothers and three stepbrothers and only one stepsister. My mom used to make me wear dresses, and she kept reminding me that I am a little girl. I still wore jeans all the time. I played baseball and climbed fences—I basically did everything my brothers did.

One day, I went to use the bathroom and one of my brothers was in there. There was a keyhole in the door, and I bent down to peek. My brother was standing up, and his back was toward me. I was shocked that my brother was standing up and using the bathroom. The very next time I used the bathroom, I tried using the toilet while standing up, only to get soaking wet. I asked my mom about it, and she sat me down and told me the best way she knew how. She spoke about boys' and girls' different body parts and the birds and the bees.

My stepbrothers and I got along very well. I was very close to my brother named Jimmy, and as kids, we did everything together. We used to walk to the zoo almost every day. There was this hill we used to go down; we named it Snake Hill because it was steep and wiggly. Now, as I look back, I realize that hill was dangerous. But being kids, we just had fun. Our sister was also with us. We would pack a lunch and spend the whole day together.

Jimmy was always there when I needed him. I loved him very much, and you will know him as I do by the time you finish this story. On the other hand, my stepsister and I did not always get along. However, I believe it had a lot more to do with me. I felt hurt, and if I was a nobody when I was around her.

When my mother and my stepfather argued, they didn't know that I was listening. My stepfather used to compare me and my sister. He would say things like, "Dottie is going to get pregnant before Belinda," because I was the outgoing one while Belinda stayed in the house most of the time. I did not know at the time he had a reason for saying things like that.

My stepdad was sneaky. I remember him giving my stepsister money anytime she would ask. We loved going to the movies; but whenever I asked for money for movie tickets, he felt around and touched in the wrong places. I never gave in, but I did not tell my mom because I was afraid. I loved my mother very much, and as a child, I knew it would hurt her. I also feared that maybe a fight would occur. I didn't want that to happen, and I did not want to be the cause of it; so, I dealt with it until her death.

My oldest brother, Bug (his nickname), went into the Air Force when I was very young; and I didn't see him again until I became a grown woman. There were times when my mom would be sitting in the living room, and a plane would fly overhead; I would hear her say, "Lord, I wonder if my child is on that plane coming home." My oldest brother made a career out of the Air Force. After serving his term, he decided to remain in the Netherlands. He got married and had two children, so my mom never did see her son again before she died.

One of my brothers had stayed in trouble for as long as I can remember. The police used to bring him home. Sometimes, he would get caught driving stolen vehicles or something. My mom would get tired of always having to go to court for him.

He had issues with my mom. My mother used to make sure that we were in the house before dark. My mom spoiled me, and I was also a little hardheaded. No, I take that back. I was hardheaded. At times, I stayed out a little longer. Oh, boy, my mom used to send one of my brothers looking for me. He always found me playing ball with the boys or jumping rope (double Dutch). He would then pick me up by my shirt and carry me home while I fussed the whole way.

He would say, "Don't you know what time it is?" I would be kicking the whole way home.

My childhood was not all bad. We had a big house with a basement. The kitchen was in the basement. I spent a good amount of time there with my mom, learning how to cook. When I was a child, I used to love rice with sugar and butter on it. I ate it by the plate!

My stepsister, brothers, and I used to hide in the basement when it was time to go to bed; then we would play games. My stepdad would come down and turn the lights on to try to find us. He never really did. We would not come out from our hiding places. When he left, then we would climb up the stairs to our rooms, laughing until we cried tears of happiness. We played games like paper dolls, hopscotch, jacks, Simon Says, hide-and-seek, and double Dutch (my favorite).

School in the sixties was fun. My best friend was Dorita. Dorita was from North Carolina. They had a huge German shepherd. I was scared of that dog. Dorita and I were friends until we lost touch with each other. I often wonder where she was, and I prayed she is doing well. We reunited as we got older and kept in touch. I loved seeing her again.

We moved to a new house on Eighteenth and T Street North Washington, and next door was this man renting a room. My mom and stepdad used to talk to him, and he seemed to be a good neighbor. I remember times when I would be out in my backyard, and he would pass me some change through the fence. I did not think much of it. However, as time went on, he continued giving me money; and I would go to the store and spend it all on candy. He later moved away, and I did not see him for a long time. Then one day, I was going to the store, and I saw him. He asked me how my mom, dad, and everyone else were doing. I was thirteen years old then.

He gave me some change, told me where he lived, and invited me over there. He said he had some things for me and wanted to give them to me. I did not go to his house that same day, but I stopped by the next day after school. I never thought he would do any harm to me because he knew my mom and stepdad, and he always treated me with respect and kindness. I would soon regret that big mistake.

He did not live far from us; it was within walking distance. I knocked on the door, and he opened it and said, "Hi. I am glad you made it. Have a seat." He asked me how my day was and what I did in school. At the same time, I was drinking an orange soda. He told me, "Put your soda down for a minute. I want to show you something." I did. At that moment, he grabbed my hands, pulled me up from the chair, and threw me on the bed.

He had one hand over my mouth; and with the other hand, he was pulling my pants off and lying on top of me with all his body weight. I was trying so hard to scream and fight back. I was crying. It did not last very long. I was hurt and bleeding. I was crying and screaming that he was going to get me pregnant. I was a virgin, and I was not ever interested in boys or sex. After that, I got myself together and went home and up to my room.

During this time, my mom was back in the hospital. I was staying with my godfather, Mr. G. He was a good person. I did not tell anyone because as I said earlier, I was scared. I did not know what to do. One day, while I was riding to school, I saw that the bus was full; so, some of us had to stand up. I was one of them. It started to get hot and stuffy all at once. Then I just blacked out.

When I came to, I was in the school nurse's office. The nurse had me go home and told me to see a doctor. Yes, I was pregnant. I was petrified and afraid. I was only in the eighth grade. I thought, *Oh, Lord, what am I going to do? I'm scared. I feel so all alone. Who can I talk to?* Then I remembered that I could talk to Jesus. My mother always told me to take care of myself and never get downhearted.

Until this day, I still wonder why I went to his house and why he did that to me. I was so stupid. *Why did I go to his house?* When I went for my first checkup, the doctor gave me a permission slip for my mom to sign. A lot of things were going through my mind. I don't know how long it was before I had to tell my godfather. I just thought about how if I gave birth to a boy, he could not be circumcised because I was underage.

I was so scared that I asked my godfather, who said he would take the papers to my mom. He first sat me down and explained to me that I had choices. I could get an abortion; or I could keep the baby, and he would be with me all the way. I told him that my mom had taught us that it is a sin to kill, so I chose to keep my baby.

During this time, my mom wanted to see me. She was still in the hospital. I had gained enough strength to go to see my mom. The first thing she had asked me was if my godfather fathered my child, and I reassured her that he wasn't the father, but JC was. She told me to take care of myself and never get downhearted. I kissed her goodbye, not knowing that was going to be the last time I would see her alive. She passed away three days later.

I blamed myself for her death. *Oh, God, what have I done? My mom is gone*, I thought. She was a living witness that God is Lord and that through Him all—and I do mean *all*—things are possible. Amen.

I thought my whole world was ending. I wanted to get in the grave with her. I cursed the Almighty. I did not understand why He took my mom from me. *What am I going to do? I do not know how to change a diaper.* There I was—all alone, pregnant, and thirteen years old. My mom had told me to stay with my godfather.

After my mom had passed, everyone in my family went their own separate way. I guess that was their way of dealing with the loss. I ended up with my godfather, and that was where I wanted to be. My godfather had raised three daughters after his wife passed, and now, he was raising five more girls who lost their parents. I would be the sixth.

My godfather taught us everything. He used to get all of us together; and he would talk to us about our bodies and how to keep them clean, about boys and how all they wanted was one thing, how to carry ourselves like young ladies, and how to give respect and demand the same from others. He told us that we were not below any human being on earth. He taught us about God and how to say our prayers and give thanks.

When it was time for me to have my baby, I knew the basics of how to care for him, thanks to my godfather. Knowing that I had such a caring person to look up to, I felt safe and secure that I would be the best that I could be.

God is Lord, and through Him, all things are possible. My son was born on November 7, 1969. I named him James Lawrence Sutton. I took him home, and I started my role as a mother. Meanwhile, JC kept his part of the bargain; he took care of James. JC and I never had physical contact again. I had five godsisters and James. He was so tiny. I had someone to love again. My only regret was that my mom never lived to see him, hold him, or love him.

On his first birthday, I gave him a birthday bash. There was this cute little African girl that was around his age who lived in our building. Her mom brought her to the party. The whole time the party was going on, the two were inseparable. Her mom used to bring her over to visit for a few minutes. She and James played well together.

No weapon formed against thee shall prosper. As to what happened to me, I never told my son about it; I never wanted him to know how he was conceived. I felt it was my choice to tell or not to tell. I, however, made the mistake of telling someone that I thought was close to me; and she told him.

Jimmy and I were very close. He always looked out for me. Whenever or wherever I needed him, he was there. He was always coming to my rescue or just hanging around. I love all my brothers and my sister very much. We were a very close family. I feel very blessed to have had them.

I remember having some good times and going to parties. I lived down the street from Meridian Hill Park. They later changed the name to Malcolm X Park. It was a beautiful place. It was very big and had a huge pond with large goldfish in it. There were some steps that had water running down them too, and it looked like a waterfall. I remember how beautiful the water looked. The park had three levels. On the top level were walkways and benches on both sides. You could see the entire park from the top level. We used to go to concerts there at night. We would sit on the grass and just enjoy the music.

Everyone got along. There are different nationalities in Washington, DC. I really miss my home the way it used to be. As a teen, I had so much to do. I miss going to the zoo, the museums, the movies, the block parties, and the picnics. I miss the walks through the park, the playgrounds, and the jogs from one side of the city to the next (from Northwest to Southeast).

I also miss going downtown to the monument and walking up all those steps to the top. I used to count them, but now I forgot how many there were. I would put my feet in the clear pool and play along the Capitol steps. I also visited the White House, lit up fireworks with my family, and went down to the monument to watch the big display of fireworks all night. Ah! It was so beautiful. I could go on and on, but I have much more to share with you.

Chapter 2

My Teen Years

· ·

We moved into an apartment building on the corner of Sixteenth and U Street Northwest. I met a lady named Maggie. She lived on the first floor. I used to go down to her apartment sometimes with my friend Eve. We would smoke marijuana and listen to music. I looked up to her. She was single, had no children, and lived in her own apartment. She also had plenty of nice male friends who sometimes would visit while we were there. These guys would join us in smoking, but they never disrespected us.

One night, Eve, I and Shelly were in Maggie's apartment. She had three male friends visiting from the Army base nearby. We all sat around smoking and drinking. One of the guys asked if we had ever tried purple haze (more commonly known as acid). Trying to pretend we had, we said yes. Each of us dropped half a tab of haze and continued partying. Then someone suggested that we all go out to the club on the Army base. Two of the guys said that they had to first stop by their house. Maggie's male friend stayed with her at her apartment; the other two guys, along with my two friends and I, rode to one of the guys' houses.

When we walked in there, I found out it was a weird tripping place. There were posters all over the walls, there was a wild type of music playing, and they had black lights on. The room we went into had this big—and I mean *big*— pipe in it. We all sat around on the floor with the pipe in the middle of us. One guy lit it up and passed it around and around. The smoke was so thick that you could cut it with a knife.

Everyone was feeling good. The guys left us in the house while they went to the store for more brew. While they were gone, Eve asked if we felt the purple haze taking effect. I told her no, and so did my other friend Shelly. One of us suggested that we find the bottle and take another tab of the acid. The three of us began searching until one of us found it. But then greed set in, and each of us dropped one whole tab. I then put some in a tissue and stuffed it in my bra. I told myself that I was going to give those to my brother Jimmy.

When the guys came back, we were ready to go home. Only one of the guys was going to drive us. However, on the way, I noticed that the guy was not on the right highway. I told the other girls about it.

One of them said to the guy, "Where are you taking us? This is not the right way."

The guy said, "One of you is going to give it up. I don't care which one."

In that instance, Eve started crying. I told her to stop crying and whispered to them that there were three of us and only one of him, that we could overpower him.

As he was driving along the highway, he stopped at this bar. He then said, "Now, we all are going in here to drink, and you all think about which one it is going to be." We got out of the car in the parking lot and started walking toward the bar. I touched my friends and signaled them to slow down and let the guy walk ahead. Once that happened, we ran. He turned around and threw his hands up at us, and then he continued to walk into the bar.

Now the three of us were stranded in Alexandria, Virginia, with no money and no coats. One of us had bedroom slippers on, and it was cold. We were afraid to call the police because our parents would be furious. One of us suggested that we take turns asking people who came out of the bar to take us home. Finally, this one guy said yes. He asked us what we were doing out in the cold at that time of the night and dressed as we were. He told us to get in his car and that he would warm it up while he went to get his partner.

We were so happy that we each dropped one more tab of acid. Suddenly, my heart dropped as I thought, *Oh, God, please let him take us home safely without harm.*

As we were driving along, listening to the music, happy to be warm and going home, I noticed that the guy was indeed on the right highway. They asked us if we smoked marijuana. One of us told them yes. Then the guy lit a joint, and we all took a puff.

A few minutes later, I started feeling strange. It seemed as though the car was floating. Then I started hearing bombs drop, like, *zoom, zoom, boosh!* At that point, I felt like I was hit. I told the driver to take me somewhere to get a cup of coffee as I thought that it might help bring me down—but it just took me up higher. Purple haze is an upper; it takes you up. My other friend said, "If you have started feeling it, I know I am next."

The guys asked what we had taken. When we told them, they yelled at us, "IF WE HAD KNOWN THAT WE WOULD NOT HAVE OFFERED YOU ALL THAT MARIJUANA!" By that time, Eve and my other friend were also tripping. We all were finally able to see the Washington

Monument. We knew we were home as we approached the city. The Fourteenth Street Bridge, the cars, the people, and the buildings all looked like toys. They did not look real. I was still hearing those bombs going off. My friend was saying that we all looked like apes.

The guys dropped us off in front of my apartment building at Sixteenth and U Street. We thanked them, and each of us went in our separate directions. I ran across the street to my godfather's job. He was the manager of the liquor store. My brother Jimmy saw me and asked, "Dottie, where have you been? We all have been looking for you. You have been gone for two days!" I learned then that my godfather was going to put out a missing person report.

I told Jimmy that I had taken some purple haze, and I reached into my bra, got the pills I was saving for him, and gave them to him. When I got to the store, my godfather told my brother to take me home and that he would be there shortly. The ambulance was called for me. Jimmy said that he was going to tell them we were at a party and that someone must have put something in my drink.

After the ambulance came, the attendants told Jimmy to watch me very closely; then they gave him two pills for me to take and instructed him not to let me out of his sight. They told him that I would go through four or five different stages. They said that I was going to experience fright, happiness, and sadness, to name a few. The pills they gave him were to help me get through my trip more quickly.

Jimmy took me to the apartment, and I laid down. He put the cover over me and told me that he was going to be right there until I got over what I was feeling. He then told me to tell him everything that I saw or went through. As I was lying down in my bed, I started to see different colors of balloons. Then I saw a pink elephant. Yes, a pink elephant. At that point, Jimmy had left to go to the bathroom. I looked over at the window, and I thought I saw my bed. It was a big fluffy bed. I got out of my real bed and climbed up to the window.

At that moment, Jimmy saved my life. He was very upset with me. You see, I lived on the fourth floor, and there were bars over my window. If the bars had not been there, I would have jumped, thinking that my bed was there. Those pills, purple haze, are deadly. I was saved by the grace of God.

I was sixteen and had a nice, shapely body. A girlfriend of mine told me that I should get a job where she worked. She said that they had an opening at the club. It was a topless go-go club, and they needed dancers. The dancers made good money. I went there with her one night and got the job. I lied and

told the manager that I was twenty-one years old. He did not ask for any identification. They just started showing me how to move my body.

I wore white patent-leather knee-high boots (called go-go boots). I also had these little tassel things covering my nipples. I worked three nights a week, and I made a lot of money. I didn't let my godfather know what I was doing; he would have never stood for that. With the money, I was able to have custom-made clothes for myself as well as my son. Sweet sixteen! I was living the life for the next couple of years. It was then that I really wanted to be independent.

When I was about to turn eighteen, I told Mr. G. that I had to go and find out how to live independently. I told him that I would never come back to live but that I would always be back to visit him. He told me that I would always have a home as long as he was living. I thanked him so much. I really appreciate all that Mr. G. did for me.

He was one of God's angels. Rest in peace, Mr. G. I love you for the life you gave me.

I moved out of Mr. G's. and moved into my high-rise apartment. I was living on the eighth floor. My apartment was laid out and had custom-made drapes—the works. The building I was living in had 120 units.

When my birthday was coming up, my girlfriends and I put the plan in motion. We had brought some pot (marijuana). I told Tammi and Tee to roll up about an ounce of pot. I baked my own cake; I mixed the pot into the batter and then put it in the oven. Meanwhile, another friend was sitting on the sofa, making a surprise for me. I had long-stemmed Austral glasses all over my apartment, and they were filled with J's (sticks of pot). I had a friend going to the liquor store to buy cases of beer, wine, liqueur, and coolers. You name it; we had it.

My party would soon begin, and I had some powder for my VIP. We also spiked the punch with tabs. I had so many people over; some were lying in the bathtub messed up. Some had to go outside onto the balcony to have some air. This was in October, and it was cold. The party was great. We had fried chicken, shrimp cocktail, tuna salad, and everything else in between. We partied for the whole month of October. Wow!

Chapter 3

My Move to Virginia

· ·

I've always provided a home for my children. I considered myself a good mom although I liked to smoke weed. I didn't want my kids to grow up in the fast lane that I'd been on. I kept my kids in check. Well, anyway, I have been thinking about my life. I was tired of getting high every day, and I was tired of my lifestyle. So, I called my cousin in Virginia, and I asked her if it would be okay if we could come down to stay with her until I find an apartment. She was overjoyed, so I put my plan in order.

I started saving my checks and sending money orders to my cousin's house in my name so that when I got there, I would have money to get an apartment. I think about three months' worth of checks were sent. I packed three suitcases—one for me and one for each of my two children. I called a cab and informed my neighbor that I was leaving and that they could have everything I left. The cab driver then took us to the bus station. Soon we were on our way to Virginia, and I knew that I had made the right choice. I felt so relieved. I knew that God wanted this for me, and I believe the move saved my life.

We made it safely to Virginia. My cousin had food ready for us to eat. *Oh, she can cook!* She had homemade mashed potatoes and pork chops with gravy and fresh greens. We ate it, and oh, the food was good! We settled in, and I got to know my new home and surroundings.

My aunt lived right behind us on JD Highway. She was a good cook too. I remember one time when she made homemade biscuits and cooked a pot of beans. She sent me out to her garden to get her a cucumber, but I mistakenly got her a squash. She said, "Child, I know you are from the city because you don't know cucumber from a squash." We both started laughing. My aunt's husband, "Huskie Cake," used to take me to the ball games at the Diamond. I had never been to a live ball game before, so I was thrilled to go.

Meanwhile, things were not going well in terms of my looking for a house, so I decided to move in with my aunt. She had a little bit more room. She gave me a big room in her home for thirty dollars a month. After I moved in, I started getting homesick. I missed DC.

I met this lady named Belinda. She had come to visit my aunt. Belinda and I became the best of friends. Then she started taking me to the clubs on Hull Street. There was one club called the Mayflower. We used to drink sixteen-ounce cans of Olde English beer and smoke marijuana. She also showed me around the city. Since she lived with her sister on JD, she was not far from my aunt's house; so, I liked going over to her house to have a good time.

When I was in my aunt's backyard one evening; this guy pulled up, came over to my aunt, and asked her to introduce me to him. Soon after, he and I started talking. He was a good man. He soon moved my children and me into an apartment; and for the next two years, we would become the best of friends for life. Even now, we still talk on the phone, touching base with each other. One day, I went over to my cousin's house, and this guy was doing some remodeling work in her kitchen. We were introduced, not knowing that later he would become my husband.

My oldest brother who lives in the Netherlands came to visit and paid my rent for one year. He took me downtown, and I got complete furnishings for my two-bedroom apartment. My bedroom set had sixteen mirrors in it. Though it cost $1,500, my brother paid for everything in cash.

You see, he had his own business and was retired from the Air Force. After he did all that for me, he went back overseas, but fortunately, we kept in touch. That was the first time I'd seen my brother in seventeen years. He looks and talks like my father. I've always looked up to him and will always respect and love him.

Later, after meeting the guy that was remodeling my cousin's house, I ran into him again. He asked to take me out, so I accepted; and for a while, we were seeing each other. He was much older than me and liked to have fun.

One night, we had been partying, smoking, and drinking. At some point, I passed out on the bed in his van. When I woke up the next morning, he told me that we were going to get married and that we were at a courthouse in North Carolina. I told him that he was crazy and that I was not going to get married to anybody. He took my hand and squeezed it with force and said, "Come on!" So we went into the building, and he told the clerk that we wanted to get our marriage license. At the same time, he was still squeezing my hand.

I tried to make faces at the lady to let her know that I did not want to get married, but I could not get her attention. I was scared.

I had not been living in Virginia long enough to know the city well, and I sure did not know where I was in North Carolina.

We got the license and went back into the van. The whole time, I was thinking that I did not want to marry that man. He rode along and stopped at three or four justices of the peace with no luck. A preacher said he could not marry us until we had counseling. At that point, I believed that there was still a good chance I would make out of this mess unmarried.

Chapter 4

My First Marriage

Drinking, Drugs, and Abuse

· ·

He was still determined to get married. I tried to convince him to wait until we got back to Virginia, but that did not work. He finally came across a preacher who would marry us. He pulled a guy off the street and promised to buy him a fifth of Wild Irish Rose if he would be a witness to the marriage.

We went before the preacher and said our "I do's." Oh, God, I did not know what was in store for me! We drove through Emporia, Virginia, his hometown while blowing the horn. He stopped at his mom's house (actually, she was not his real mom but the lady who raised him). Then we headed back to Richmond. I was so sad and scared that I kept asking myself how I could have done this. I blamed myself for drinking and falling asleep. I did not know at the time that he put something in my drink. It turned out that this was a setup from the very beginning. Being young and dumb then, how could I have known?

We made it back to my apartment, which was now *our* apartment. He put the marriage certificate in a frame and hung it over the bed. Later that day, I found out that he had about six or eight children. Soon after, I discovered that I was not his first wife but his third. I took the marriage license down from the wall and tore it up. After one or two weeks, I kicked him out of my apartment.

This man was crazy! Whenever he saw me on the street, he always wanted to fight me. At one point, we got back together. Things were fine for a while. But then he started smoking pot daily, in addition to his drinking habit. I remember a time he abused me so much that I got to the point where I was tired, I bought a special long-nosed .38 caliber pistol and a whole box of bullets. I hid them in a hatbox in my closet. By the grace of God, my husband found it. My plan was self-explanatory. I thank my God that it never happened.

My husband and I later separated. Our relationship was on and off again. He had access to my bank account, and he took everything out of it. My oldest brother, the one who lived in the Netherlands, would send me money every month to make sure that my kids and I were well taken care of. I had accumulated about ten thousand dollars in my checking account, which I foolishly put in a joint account after my husband kept nagging me to do so.

One day, I went to the store to buy groceries. I wrote a check for fifty dollars to cover the amount for food. About two weeks later, two nicely dressed men were knocking at my door. They asked for my name and showed me a check. They asked me if I wrote the check, and I told them that I did. Then they told me that the check bounced.

I said, "What do you mean 'bounced'?"

They said, "Didn't you know you don't have any money in your account?"

I just stood there in shock for a moment. I told them that I did have money in my account, then I went upstairs to get my checkbook and showed them the amount I knew I had. One of the guys told me that they were supposed to arrest me; but since I really did not know that my money was gone, they would not lock me up, if I signed the warrant saying that I will appear in court. I agreed to do that with tears rolling down my cheeks. I then knew that all my money was gone…and so was my husband.

My ex-husband left town and hid for nearly a year. I believe he went back to Emporia, Virginia. When I saw him again, I confronted him about cleaning out my bank account. His exact words were "I used you for what you were worth." Those words haunted me for years.

I had many bad memories from my relationship with that man. I recall the time when I left him and moved into an apartment on the other side of town. My ex-husband found out where I lived. He saw me coming out of the apartment with my children and a male friend. He wanted me to take him back. At that time, our relationship was over for good. I told him no, so he yelled at me, "B****! I SHOULD SET YOUR A** ON FIRE!" I really did not think much of it at the time because my friend and I were on our way to DC, to take the children for summer vacation.

On the drive to DC, we noticed that the "hot" light kept turning on in the car. My friend said he did not know what was wrong with the car. He checked the oil and put water in the car, so it should not have been running hot. We made it up there to drop the children off and then headed back to Richmond. When we arrived, my friend suggested that I go to his sister's house to lie down because I had a headache. He was going to check on my apartment.

When he got back, I took one look at him and knew that something was wrong. I could see it all over his face. He said, "Dee, I don't know how to tell you this, but your apartment is burned down to the ground! Everything in it is gone." I told him to take me there. When we drove up to where my apartment was, surely it was burned to the ground. There was nothing left.

I fell on my knees and cried out, "LORD, OH, LORD, WHY ME?" Then I started saying the Lord's Prayer, "Our Father, who art in Heaven, hallowed be thy name…" I never felt so hurt in my life. One of my furnishings was less than a couple of months old. My brother purchased everything for me and my children, and it was all gone. The thought about how my ex-husband had made that statement, about setting me on fire…

When I spoke to the fire chief, he told me that at about 2:30 a.m., someone threw a Molotov cocktail through my window. My ex-husband had intended for my children and I to be in the house. He had all intentions of killing us that day. Thank you, God! Thank you! I can get more material things, but for the children, I can't replace them. God, I thank thee!

That so-called marriage was on and off again for about six years. I found out that he was into Roots, Voodoo, and he was working Roots on me. He was giving me something through my smokes. I also found out he was trying to kill me because he had a big life insurance policy on me. We were separated many years before I finally filed for divorce. I had to track him down to obtain his signature, and after that, it was truly the end.

Chapter 5

My Abusive Relationships

· ·

When discussing abusive situations, I must go back to my first marriage. During the course of my first marriage with my ex-husband, he broke my nose twice. I have had too many black eyes to count. On my birthday, he had promised to take me out. I waited a day for him to come home, just for him to bust my lip and break my nose.

Following the breakup of my marriage, I began dating a younger guy, the relationship went on for about four years. His name was Jason, and as it turned out he was very obsessed with me. I found myself in another abusive relationship. I really felt that he would kill me. I felt as if there was no way out. He drove me to the point of desiring to take my own life and the life of my daughter. I was tired of all the abuse. I had very low self-esteem, and I felt that no one would take care of my little girl like I would.

With Jason, I could not go to the bathroom without him following me and asking me what was taking so long. If I would look out the window, he would ask me, "Who are you looking at?" If I went to the store, he would keep an eye on the clock. If I did not return in thirty minutes, he would come looking for me. On the weekend when I would catch a cab to a friend's house, he would arrive at my friend's house walking on foot before I would arrive in the cab. He walked nearly twenty miles on foot from one part of town to another.

One night, I was running away from him. I tripped on something in the street and fell. He quickly caught up with me and shouted, "B****! You are trying to run? I'm gonna make sure you don't walk no more!" He took my foot and twisted it. I heard my bones crack. He then walked away. I stumbled while trying to get up and hobbled away. I could not feel any pain then because I was drunk, but I eventually made it home. The next morning, trying to stand up getting out of bed I screamed at the top of my lungs. I then looked down at my foot. It was so big. I screamed, "Call 911! I need to go to the hospital!" The abuser who did this to me ended up taking me to the hospital.

If you have ever been physically abused, you know what I am talking about. This guy's personality would go from day to night. He acted like nothing ever happened. When I got to the emergency room, the doctors said that my right ankle was broken in several places, and they wanted to put metal rods in my ankle. I told them no, so they put a cast on my foot instead and gave me some pain pills, and then they let me go home. I was too scared to tell anyone what happened.

So many incidents occurred with Jason. I was really scared of him. I had to change jobs so many times because of him. I was a housekeeper; he knew what line of work I did. He would get the yellow page phone book and call every hotel, motel, and inn until someone told him that I did work for them. Other times, he would ask my so-called friends, and they would tell him where I moved or worked. Another time, he pushed me off the porch, and I ended up hitting my head. I was knocked unconscious. He also broke my nose, tried to knock my teeth out, and was always stalking me. My face was so beaten up by this man that I did not even recognize myself when I looked in the mirror.

Another time, I was standing in a parking lot talking with some friends when suddenly, Jason jumped out of a car, grabbed me from behind, and pointed a sawed-off shotgun at me and my friends. Another one of my friends pulled out their pistol, Jason pointed the sawed-off at them, telling them don't even try it. As he backed away, toward the car with me in tow, he pushed me inside. There was another guy driving.

The guy drove us to a hotel, Jason displayed the rifle again and kept clicking it, successfully putting fear in me. He told me that he should kill me. I was really scared, but I kept my cool and tried to act as if everything was fine. To calm him down, I told him that we could get back together and that I would meet him at a certain time later that day. He bought it, thinking everything was ok even though there was no truth to what I had said. I just wanted to get away from him. I know that the Lord and his angels were sent to save my life. By God's grace, I was. Thank you, Lord.

When I met this guy, he did not have a record; but by the time the relationship was over, he had a long one. When he poured kerosene on me, he should have been charged with attempted murder. Instead, they charged him with assault and gave him four months in jail. (Yes, only four months!)

I went to a hideaway house for abused women and children. My little girl and I went there for a while. That place is a God-sent. Any woman who is in an abusive relationship: please know there is help. I did not have anyone or anywhere to turn, but this safe-haven organization came and picked us up. We met them at a certain place, they drove a little bit from that place. Not even the drivers know where the hideaway house is located.

When we walked into the house, there were others there just like me. In worse shape than I was. I had my own room for my child and myself. There was plenty of food and clothes. They can even get your children into school without any papers. They will relocate you if you want so you can start fresh. These programs for abused women are the best. You will feel safe because they do everything possible to keep you safe, and the best thing is no one knows where you are. You also have group talks and learn, as I did, that abusive men all have common ways; they all do the same things.

Never believe them when they say that they are sorry or that they love you. Abusers must acknowledge they have a problem, want to make a change, seek help, and be able to repent before God. Otherwise, nothing will change. In fact, in my case, things got worse. There were times I looked in the mirror, and I could not believe what I saw. My face was so messed up. I just knew that I would not be the same again. Oh, yes, the physical bruises went away somewhat; but the mental scars stayed.

After leaving the hideaway house, I did not relocate and yes, Jason found me. One night, I do not remember what happened to have caused his abusive behavior, but Jason started beating me outside of his friend's house. It was around seven or eight o'clock in the morning. Someone walked by and said, "Man, what are you doing?" Jason simply said, "Nothing," and just walked away. I ran back into the house and got my daughter and started walking toward JD Highway.

As I started walking along the highway, I told Niva that we would be better off in Heaven. I held Niva's hand, kneeled, and wrapped my arms around her. I closed my eyes, waiting for the end. Suddenly, Niva's dad came and snatched her out of my arms, then he grabbed me and pulled us out of harm's way. Back then, all I could think was, *Oh, God, how did I get to this point? Help me, Lord! Help me!*

Jason did get five years in prison. Finally, that was my way out of the abusive relationship. The system had not always worked, but now they are so serious about abuse and stalking that they made a law around it. So please do not think there is no help. There is more help now than ever before.

Chapter 6

My Second Marriage

The Good, the Bad, and the Unfaithful

. . . .

I had been getting to know this guy whose nickname was Wallace for almost four years. He did some work for me, and after that, we just started talking and seeing each other. When we got together, he treated me how a woman is supposed to be treated. He loved my children, and that really made me fall in love with him.

We lived together for about three years, and my children grew to love him as well. Unfortunately, there was a lady in his life from his past with whom I had thought that he had broken all ties with. I did not know then that I was in for a rude awakening. This lady was old enough to be his grandmother. She would come around all the time. He was still messing around with her; and I was oblivious to it all, mostly because I was still drinking and really did not see it (or perhaps I simply did not want to).

He was doing his thing; and then one Mother's Day, Wallace promised me that he was going to take me out for the occasion. I got dressed up, then I waited and waited. After waiting for a long time, I got angry and decided to pack all his things. Afterward, I had someone give me a ride to take his things to his dad's home. On the way to his dad's, I spotted him. He was not alone. He was walking down the street holding hands with this girl. It was not the older woman but someone else.

I jumped out of the truck and went after the girl, hollering at her, saying, "He's my man!" I went toward him and told him to give me my keys as I started to hit him. The person who drove me literally picked me up and put me back in the car. I was hurt. I really loved him. Then my drinking habit began to worsen from that point on. When I arrived back home, I was crying uncontrollably; and all I could think about was payback.

My oldest daughter came over and said that she wanted to take me out, so I got in the car. At that point, I was not in my right state of mind, and she knew it. My daughter took me to Westbrook Psychiatric Hospital. When I got there, I knew that it was the best place for me. I had stayed there for a little less than two weeks before I was back in my right state of mind. The effects of the booze and weed wore off. I eventually realized that what I was thinking about doing to him was wrong. I am grateful to my God and to Monica for keeping me safe. Monica kept her sister during my stay.

After I got out of the hospital, I went home. My mind was not on that man at all. I spent time with my daughters, mostly with Niva because Monica had her own place and worked all the time. Niva and Monica are ten years apart.

Much later down the road, I met another man, who was much older than I was. I felt comfortable enough to talk to him about what had happened in my last relationship, how I felt betrayed, and how much happier I was after everything. This guy was good to me, and everything was going great—that is, until Wallace came back around, and I fell for him again. This time, he asked me to marry him. *Why now, just when I had gotten my mind off him and was starting to do much better?*

My new friend begged me not to marry him. "Please do not marry him," he said. "I will pay your rent and bills. That way, you can keep your money to do whatever." I told him that I was not going to; but deep down in my heart, I had already decided that I was going to marry Wallace. I wanted a real family for Niva's sake, and I also wanted to belong. I was also fixated on how I was getting older, and I wanted to have an "Until death do us part" man. Last but not least, I wanted security. Wallace was a military man. Besides, the older guy was married!

I spent my last night with my new friend, knowing that I was going to be a married woman within a week. I then went forward with my plans to get married at my house. The pastor came to perform the ceremony.

Things seemed to go smoothly for a while. However, he soon started staying out at night and not coming home from work. He would not call to see if I needed anything or if I was all right. We moved to the north side of town.

Shortly after I had my first panic attack, the day my oldest daughter was sentenced to 179 years in prison. We had only been married a short time when that happened. I had just come home on bond for being locked up and was trying to get my life back in order. I had gotten to the point where I could not work anymore. In one year, I filed seven W-2 forms. I tried to work, but I had to stop because of my illness. The doctors were trying to find out what was wrong with me, I was scared because I didn't know.

I needed my husband more than ever. Every time I was with Wallace no matter where we were and I got that feeling like I was going to have an attack, he would leave me alone, scared, and confused. To this day, I don't know why he always left me during these attacks. He could be driving down the street, and I would say, "Wallace, I'm beginning to feel strange again." Wallace would pull over and would go into any store he saw at the time, and he would not come out until he thought it was over. He was never there for me—not even at my son's funeral. It was God and his grace that watched over Niva and me during those times.

Finally, the doctor found out that I was having anxiety attacks. It was due to the stress I had endured throughout my entire life thus far. Your mind can take only so much before it cracks (my opinion). Now I can't work anymore. When I was working, I helped pay our bills, buy food, etc. One day, my husband told me that he had a moving job to do on a Saturday. He drove tractor-trailers at his regular job, and he was going out of town to move someone back to Virginia. Wallace told me that he would be back late Saturday night and that he would have some extra money when he gets back. I said okay.

The next time I saw my husband was two months later. He abandoned me and my children. He left knowing that I didn't have a job, any food, a way to pay bills, or much of anything. I called his job and his father's house a trillion times. The guy who answered the phone at his job said that he had been coming to work every day and that he gave him all my messages. But I know him. He was avoiding me with no explanation whatsoever as to why he left me with nothing. I was convinced that another woman had to be involved, and soon everything was getting cut off.

My oldest daughter and I did temp work. I was sick, but I had to do something. We ate noodles and did construction work. It was hard to find a job in a state that had tarnished our name, even though all charges were dropped and erased. One day Wallace came over with tears in his eyes. He admitted that he was wrong, that he was sorry, and that it wouldn't happen again. He told me that he left me for a married woman. Her husband was in the service. I believed in my vows, and I loved my husband. So, I forgave him.

We moved to another section of town. We rented a nice two-bedroom bungalow. I was totally dependent on him for support. Monica asked me to sign up for disability, but I did not want to. I was so set on being independent and having my own, so I just could not see it. But I soon signed up for it. It would be ten long months before I would receive my first check. They were the longest ten months of my life.

He really showed me what I meant to him. During this time, I was waiting to be approved for SSI. Again, he stopped coming home on payday and stayed out all night long. One time, I saw his credit card statement. It showed payments for dinner at a restaurant I had never been to. One morning, he came home with his underwear on backwards (the tag was in the front, and the opening was in the back). I gathered that he was in a hurry. Another time, he came home with women's underwear on (there were flowers all over them). I guess that meant she had his.

I endured all this and more during those ten months. I was faithful to him. I kept the home clean and had his dinner ready although most of the time, I ended up throwing it away because he was never there to eat. I would fix it for him regardless of what time of night or day. I am not perfect, but I can say I was a good wife to him. I was so hurt that when I got the news that I'd been approved, I said, "What's good for the goose is good for the gander." I was tired of him running around on me. I started going out on Friday and coming home on Sunday. I did it three weekends straight.

The third weekend, when I got home, he was there. He asked me to get some tools from his toolbox for him. I didn't know what type of tools he wanted, so I told him to get them himself. He called me a name. At that time, I was looking in the refrigerator and had my back turned. He hit me; and I fell to the floor, screaming at him. He picked me up and pulled me into the bedroom, hollering at me and saying all kinds of bad things. I called out to a girlfriend to go get my daughter next door and call the police.

The police came and told him to leave and cool down. They advised me to take out a warrant, so that was what I did. I got a restraining order for him to stay away from me for one year. I have asked him to reconcile about three times. All three times, he said, "No! What the hell! It's all for the best. You can't change a hoe." That's the way we split. It's been twenty-six years; until this day, we are still split up. Wallace has filed for a divorce.

Chapter 7

My Near-Death Experiences

· ·

I was in DC. My brother Jimmy and I have always been together. I was living in the downtown area in this apartment building, and I was supposed to testify against my next-door neighbor on a case. Jimmy and I were going to this African party that night that was being held in the same building. Later that night, we went to the party and had a good time. We got back to my apartment at about two o'clock in the morning and crashed. Jimmy fell asleep on the sofa, and I laid across my bed. We were both drunk.

I remember being pulled straight up from my clothes until I was standing on my feet. I was pulled toward the kitchen to the stove. I started swaying over the stove, and then I was pulled toward my front door. I started turning the doorknob, but it was jammed. I kept trying to open the door; and then all at once, the door opened. *Whoosh!* Smoke came gushing in. I slammed the door shut and screamed, "Fire! Fire!"

Jimmy rushed toward me as we started getting James and Monica (my babies) and headed for the fire escape by my bedroom window. I lived on the fourth floor. Jimmy had one baby in his arm, and I had the other. As I was behind Jimmy, he was screaming and kicking out windows, letting the people know to get out of the apartment building. By the time we got to the ground floor, the fire department was already there. My brother looked at me and asked, "Dottie, how did you wake up?"

I started to explain to him what had happened—that something pulled my clothes, that I could see my blouse sticking out, but that I didn't see anyone pulling on me. Jimmy looked at me and said, "Dottie, that was nobody but Momma." I just shook my head and said, "Yeah."

Thank the Lord the fire chief found the cause (awesome)! He told us that someone had poured gas on my door rug, down the steps to the next level, all the way toward the girl's apartment door rug. In that apartment lived the person I was to testify against. Instantly, the girl and I knew who did this, and we told the fire chief. Then they arrested him and gave him the maximum sentence.

I thank the Lord for saving my life more than once, more than twice. As the old saying goes, "The Lord looks out for babies and fools." He knows that I have been a fool so many times before. I praise your name, Lord. I praise you, the Almighty.

I was in Virginia, during the time of my drugging, and I was close to this girl named Kim. We were good friends. By then, she had been doing drugs for about ten years. At that time, I had slowed down a little from drinking. We used to hang out together every day. I would go with her to get her drugs, and then we would go back to her place, then she would cook it up. I would be sitting down, drinking my beer. I would sit through her shooting it up while she would tell me never to do it.

One day, we went to get some cocaine; and when we got back to the house, she cooked it up. For some reason, I said that I wanted to try it. She thought I was joking, but I told her I was serious. She fixed the needle, and I shot it in with her help. I had been around it enough to know what to do, but really, I did not know.

A few seconds later, I did not feel anything, so I backed the needle up about two or more times. In that instance, my heart started racing. I mean, it was beating so fast and so hard that my eyes started rolling back into my head. I could hear Kim saying, "Don't go out on me." At that time, she started helping me up and took me to the back porch. Suddenly, a big book flashed in front of me.

The pages that were flashing in front of me, were of different encounters that I had from my childhood to adulthood. All of a sudden, I went through this dark tunnel, and I saw a bright light. The light was so bright that it hurt to look directly into it. At that time, I knew that I was dying from an overdose of cocaine. I could not talk because my mouth was so numb from the drugs, but for some reason, I could still think in my head. I thought, *Lord, don't take me now. My kids need me.*

Right then and there, I came back from the tunnel. The pages in the book flipped backwards, and I did not know anything from that point until I woke up at the hospital with the doctor looking down over me. The first thing he said was, "You are one lucky lady." I just stared at him because I really did not know if I was alive or dead. He said, "You had enough cocaine in your system to kill two people." Lord, I thank you for answering my prayer!

For about five months after I got out of the hospital, my chest hurt. Just inhaling and exhaling was painful. My heart ached as well.

Anyone who does drugs knows that cocaine will bust your heart open if you overdose. I am blessed and thankful.

I also recall a time when my abusive boyfriend Jason, whom I mentioned earlier, was walking down from the gas station, getting some kerosene for our heaters. It was in the wintertime; and like I've mentioned earlier, he was like day and night. Jason started arguing with me about something I don't remember what; but then all at once, Jason hit me. I fell, hitting my head on the ground, knocking me out cold. As I was lying there, I could smell and feel something cold being poured on me, my skin was burning. At that moment, my eyes opened; and I heard him say, "I'M GONNA SET YOU'RE A** ON FIRE."

Jason was pouring kerosene on me, and then he started flicking on his lighter. However, each time he flicked it, it would not light up. All at once, something or someone pulled me up clean out of my shoes. I looked up and saw my cousin's house straight ahead. I ran and ran, never looking back. I got to my cousin's house bursting through the door, screaming, "HE'S TRYING TO KILL ME!" They called the police, rescue came, and I went to the hospital. For this attempt on my life, he was only given four months. Once again, I say, "Thank you, Lord."

The Lord saved me another time. I was living in JW (another part of town). Wallace, myself, my daughter Niva, and her pet rabbit went upstairs to her room to go to sleep. I wanted to sleep downstairs on the sofa, but I went upstairs.

We were all asleep when I suddenly heard Wallace say, "Dottie! Dottie, get up! There's smoke everywhere." I jumped up. Niva was in the room with us. I got the window up and started to throw Niva out the window when I heard someone say, "Don't throw her! We are here." The fire department was there with the ladder up to the window. Then the fireman grabbed my daughter and carried her down the ladder. After they rescued Niva, they came and rescued me and then Wallace.

When Niva screamed, "MY RABBIT," they rescued her rabbit as well. I thought, *Thank you, Lord. We are all safe*, as we were sitting down and breathing through an oxygen mask. This man came over and spoke to me. He said that he was the one who called the fire department. Apparently, he had just gotten off from work and had seen smoke coming from my apartment.

I was looking up at him, and I said, "Thank you! Thank you so much."

I turned my head toward Wallace and said, "Did you hear what that man said? He was the one who called 911."

Wallace looked at me and said, "What man? I didn't see any man."

I said, "You had to."

At that moment, I got up and started looking around for this man, yet I never found him.

A couple of months later, I asked Wallace again, and he said the same thing: he didn't see any man standing there talking to me. Lord, Lord, I thank you! I do believe each of us has our own guardian angel, and that night, ours were sent to save our lives. Thank you, Father. I love you!

Chapter 8

The Day My World Fell Apart

· ·

We went to court on December 22nd, to try and get my bond reduced. My lawyer asked the judge to lower my bond to $3,500. Which meant I would have to pay $300 to get out. The judge said no, which was not a surprise to me. As it stands, my bond remained the same at $14,000. I need $1,400 to get out. I thanked my lawyer for doing everything he could to get me out of here before Christmas. I felt so hurt and disappointed. I cried some, and then I just pulled myself together. Then reality hit. I realized that the devil was playing his part. I suppose that was his plan from the start.

Well, it is Christmas Eve, and I am still here. I am now out of isolation and in the population with about fifty other females. I can watch television, smoke my cigarettes, and use the phone anytime I want until eleven o'clock at night. I have met a whole lot of friends. I know all of them know my situation, and they are all right with it.

They also changed my uniform color from orange, which represents a felony to yellow which represents a misdemeanor, which are the charges I am being charged with. The way I finally got into the population at the jail was through this girl I met in isolation. I asked her to write a letter. I told her what to write, and she knew to whom to write the letter to, so I can get answers—and it worked!

I thank God each day because without Him, I am lost. On this Christmas Eve, I feel very depressed. I am trying to make it. I love Wallace and Niva so much. It hurts me more than I can say. This is a very painful time for me. Only God knows.

I talked to my daughter Niva the other day. I am going to call her again today and wish her a Merry Christmas. God knows how I long to be with them. I do not want any visitors on Christmas Day. It may sound selfish. But I just cannot stand to see them leave.

The most painful part is seeing them leave afterward. I do not want them to see me break down, so I have asked them not to visit me on Christmas. Somehow, someday, and in some way, I will be free. I refuse to give up. I have been reading the Bible and praying that I will get something out of it that will keep me surviving.

Hebrews 13:6 says, "So we say with confidence, the Lord is my helper. I will not be afraid what can man do to me?" Each time I feel depressed or lonely, I look in my Bible and read from that scripture. I am asking the good Lord to help me make it through this holiday.

They indicted Monica on fourteen counts of accessory before the fact, which carries the sentence of life in prison. Lord, take care of my child. What is going to happen next? I still did not know who the person was testifying against me. After the holiday, I will find out.

Ben goes back to court on January 20, 1995. They both are still in Riker's Island, a prison in New York; and I am still locked up. It has been one month and seven days now.

December 28, 1994

Christmas is over, and I am thankful for that. It was a very sad day for me, but I made it through with the help of the good Lord.

I am still holding on in this hellhole. The days seem shorter since I have been in the population. I have told my husband to sell all my furniture, the washing machine, the televisions, and everything else he can sell to get me out of here. He said that he would do it; and with the help of the good Lord, I pray to be out by this weekend because the first of January is this Sunday. On New Year's Day, I want to be with my daughter and husband; but if not, then I will just get down on my knees and thank the Lord for letting me live to see another day, a New Year.

I hope and pray that Monica is up in New York being strong and praying. I love her so much. I pray the good Lord will bless and strengthen her to tell the truth. I know deep down in my heart that she is innocent. My child did not have anything to do with this mess, regardless of how much the news media is blowing everything out of proportion. I dislike the news media. They are the reason why the world is thinking the way they are, and we were already convicted without a trial. God will make a way for us.

My little girl was so happy about Christmas. She told me she loved everything that my friend and I bought for her, the dolls and everything. I love her so much. All three of my children, I miss and love so dearly. I dislike Ben for what he did to my daughter and my family. What type of person is he? But who am I to judge?

I am still waiting for January 20 to see what will happen in New York with Ben. My life will never be the same again. I'm also dealing with going to court on January 19 for my son. I took a warrant for his arrest because he assaulted me at my home. This is the third time he has done this; but the first time, I decided to take action. I know that he has a sickness. He is a drug addict, and I just want him to get some help.

I met a few people in here, a girl named Sammie, Ruby, Lyn, and Rose. Sammie is a nice girl, we talk about everything, and we plan on keeping in touch. Sammie goes home in a month. She has a little girl like I do. She will be missed. We laugh and trip off Ruby, Lyn is a trip also. Rose, the girl I met in isolation, is still good to me. She is transferring tomorrow, and she will be missed. God help us all!

January 3, 1995

I got a visit from Niva and Wallace. They look so good. My daughter is getting taller every time I see her. Lord, I need you. I know you are working it out, but sometimes the devil tries to get in my head and discourage me. But he is a liar.

I am living day by day. It is getting harder and harder to deal with my situation. I have not felt good for a week. I have been having headaches, fevers…and I just feel weak. I saw the nurse the other day. She checked my blood pressure and said it was high, and she wants me to see the doctor on Monday.

I have not had any problems with my blood pressure for about six or seven years. The nurse said it was from stress and the pressure that I am under right now. When I see the doctor, I know he is going to put me on blood pressure pills. Lord, I do not want to get sick in here. They'd rather wait until you are almost dead before they give you treatment.

I feel a little bit better today. This morning, my friend Sammie and I were talking about hair when Ruby started some stuff with this other girl. Something she said had me in it. I started to argue with her as well, but I know that I am more intelligent than that. I kept my cool and told myself, "Put it in the Lord's hands." Meanwhile, the devil is still working, trying to get me back into isolation. But I am too smart for him. I am determined to outsmart him.

I want to go home so bad. I'm praying to God to please help me. My daughter Monica went to court in New York. Now, she is going back on January 17. I got a friend of mine to write her a letter. I have not heard anything from her yet, but I am praying she will write me back and let me know that she is all right. I have not been able to talk or get in touch with her since all this started. I think about, pray, and feel for my beloved daughter. I love her.

Monica has been charged with fourteen felonies before the fact. I know and believe my daughter did not have anything to do with this. They are railroading us because we know Ben. I resent what he has done to our lives. I hope we can start fresh someday, somewhere. The Lord is my shepherd, and I shall not want.

Since I have been in here, I have been taking all kinds of drugs to keep myself sane. I only eat one soup a day. I have no appetite. All I want is to be free. I try not to worry or get upset because of my blood pressure. But it is very hard being in a place like this. Oh, God, please help me! This is more than I can bear. This morning, I went into the bathroom; and this girl was sitting on the commode, squeezing something down from her private. She had tissue paper full of blood on it. It made me sick. You do not know who has what in this disgusting place.

There are only three showers, three toilets, and three sinks with sixty-six females on this tier. I am being as careful as I can be, but it is not enough. I just need to get out of here. Please, God, have some good news for me. When I see Wallace and my daughter today, I will be so happy. I just cannot take it anymore.

I sent for my lawyer last week. I have not heard from him. I also must go to court on Monday for James, my son. It breaks my heart to go through so much pain. I do not know why my life has been changed around like this. I have never intentionally hurt anyone.

My friend Sylveta has a phone now. We talk on the phone almost every day. She is the best. Today, I have not called her because I am angry with her, I am under a lot of stress and tension. The least thing that she says will hurt my feelings. She is a close and dear friend; I have never had a friend like her. I will call her tonight before I go to sleep.

January 13, 1995

I went to court this past week for my son James. I took a warrant out on him way before all these problems started. The judge gave him six months with three years suspended over his head. What a shame… mother, daughter, and son locked up in jail. Only the Lord knows. I had to do what I had to do. My own son wants to beat me and destroy my property. I feel sorry because I know it's not him.

My lawyer wants to get evidence from the district attorney starting with the person willing to testify against me. The district attorney did not have anything better to do than to put it off until February 6, 1995. The district attorney does not have anything on me because I have not done anything wrong. Well, my lawyer told me that the district attorney "needs me more than they thought." Whatever that means…I do not know anything, and I am not going to testify against anyone. I do not know what the district attorney is talking about. It is getting closer to the time for Ben to go back to court.

January 18, 1995

I am still dealing with jail life. I have seen many females leave and some return as if this was their home. This will never be home for me. Some days, I am depressed, and some days I am good. I got a visit from my husband, my daughter, Sylveta, and her two boys. I was very happy to see them. I love them all very much.

Niva has grown. Oh, God, how I miss her! She was having problems where she was staying, but now, she is doing much better. Wallace looks good but worried. I could see it on his face. The gray hairs on his head are showing much more clearly. Sylveta looks great. I can tell she has been taking really good care of herself. I think she may be pregnant. Time will tell.

Oh, God, how I miss them all! It hurts so much to see them leave without me. Monica went to court on January 17. They gave her another court date for later this month. Ben is going to court on January 20. I pray they bring him back here so I can get my life back on track. I do not know how much more I can bear.

Yesterday makes two months since I have been in here. It seems like two hundred years. Believe me. I do not deserve this. The low-income housing office had the nerve to send me a summons to go to court on February 3rd for not paying rent. Tell me. How can I pay rent while I am still locked up? This place they call Virginia sucks.

Well, now, I cannot call and talk with my daughter. Her aunt put a block on the telephone. I am supposed to go to court tomorrow for a motion to get whatever evidence the district attorney has against me. My lawyer told me I do not have to be in court because it is just a matter for which he must attend. I feel like I am being railroaded all the way around. He said the district attorney is typing it up; and as soon as he gets it, he is going to give me a copy. It does not make sense to put me through all of this. I do not have anything to do with it. It is just because I am Monica's mother.

Monica and Ben are supposed to be coming to Virginia. I pray that it happens. Lord knows I am so tired of playing this waiting game and not knowing my fate. Dear Lord, please help me. I am tired of being locked up in this jail. I am giving all my problems to the Lord. The Lord is still working it out for me.

I wrote Monica in Riker's Island, New York. Guess what? She wrote me too. Thank you, Jesus! My baby is doing okay. She said it seems hopeless, but I am telling her to pray—pray as if she has never prayed before and truly mean it. My child is innocent. I never believe that she had anything to do with it. I love her so much. I am looking forward to seeing her and being with her so much, even if it is in here—jail. She did not go to New York with him willingly. Ben threatened our lives, me, and her sister if she did not go. He meant it, and I believe it.

My son is upstairs in the same jail. I wrote him a letter and sent him a cross to wear and a true poem about drugs. I told him he needs help and that this is a chance to get clean. Being locked up behind bars is the only way he can get clean and away from the streets.

Life in jail is hell. There have been girls leaving and coming back here so much; it is a sickness. Valentine's Day is coming soon. I made my daughter, Sylveta, and my man Valentine's cards. I wish I could be with them.

I still go to see the jail psychiatrist. I am still taking pills to help me sleep and deal with my nerves and miserable life here in this jail. I just do not know how much more I can take. Sylveta has stuck by me through all of this. She is a very dear friend; I am forever grateful for her.

My baby daughter is going through some changes. She wants her mom home, and she is so lonely. I want to be with her. It is a big burden on my child. It hurts me so much to see what she is going through, and I cannot be there for her. Oh, God, she is missing me. I should be there for her. On February 17, it will be three months that I have been locked up like a caged animal. I just cannot take any more of this.

Something must give. I am going to close for now because I was supposed to call Sylveta at 12:30 p.m., and it is now 1:45 a.m. Finally, the judge lowered my bond. I got out! Hallelujah! Thank you, thank you, Jesus! Oh, how I love thee! I stayed with friends for a while, and then soon we moved into a home.

I continued to work for a cleaners on Hull Street. I spent a lot of time with Niva. I had promised her a home with a white picket fence and a puppy. I was going to keep my promise. I worked, kept in touch with my lawyer, and kept up with what was going on with my daughter's case.

A little time has passed. They tried Ben and Monica the same day in different courtrooms. Also on that same day, my youngest daughter was graduating from elementary school, going into middle school. Oh, God, how can I be in two places at the same time? I knew it wasn't a good idea to be at the court, so I was going to see Niva graduate. My mind was racing. I was trying to be happy for Niva; and at the same time, I was hurting for Monica. I got through the graduation. Niva was beautiful. We all rushed to her aunt's house to listen to the news about Monica. I can't explain how I was feeling.

We all sat down, and the TV was already on. Oh, God, my baby was given 179 years with ten years suspended. I was numb. I just want to go to the cemetery to find my father's grave. I want to be alone. I just want to talk to my dad. I need him so badly. We looked and looked, yet we couldn't find his grave. When we began to leave, I started feeling sick. Fortunately, there was a hospital close by. Wallace drove us there, and I went in. When I got inside, I started shaking uncontrollably. That was the day I had my first panic attack.

It took a while before I knew what was wrong with me. About a year later, it was time for me to go back to court. Two days before my court date, my lawyer told me that the district attorney was dropping all charges against me, I was "INNOCENT", and they cleared my record. I praise your name, Jesus! I never gave up on you and never lost my faith. Now I know what my mom meant when she said, "Never get downhearted."

Monica did three and a half years in prison; they housed her out-of-state in South Carolina, five hours away from home. One day, they woke her up in the middle of the night. They told her, "Pack your bags. You are free to go." The state where her charges occurred had sent a car to pick her up. They were waiting outside. My child was "INNOCENT;" all her charges were dropped, and her record was erased. *Oh, My God! Thank you, Lord.* Of course, they told her she could not discuss or talk about it.

Ben got the death penalty, and he was killed six years later by lethal injection. It has been over twenty years now since all this took place, and I thank God for being such an awesome God. Amen!

Chapter 9

The Death of My Only Son

· ·

It's been twenty-one years on October 25, 2008, since the death of my son. As I mentioned in an earlier chapter, my son and I "grew up" together. He was around four or five years old before he had any siblings. As he became a young man, we became friends. I could sit and talk to him about anything, and he did the same with me. I used to share some of my experiences with him and information about the streets. I did not want him to be a fool or to follow in my footsteps. The very things that I warned him about were the very things that he himself did. My son had a good heart, and he was a hardworking person, like his mom. I loved him dearly although he did not think so.

He met his first child's mother, and things were fine for a while. Then he met another woman named Tootsie, who broke up their relationship. I began to hear that James had started smoking marijuana. Tootsie told him he did not have to work because she had enough money to take care of him, so he took her up on her offer. They stayed together for about seven or eight years. During their relationship, Tootsie and my son had a beautiful baby girl.

Not long after that, he himself started selling drugs and smoking marijuana laced with cocaine. He got to the point where he was strung out on drugs, stealing from her, lying, and no longer being responsible. Tootsie had enough, and she told him that he had to go. Before all this began to happen, my son had gotten stabbed half an inch away from his heart. I will never forget it.

I was working when I got the telephone call telling me to come to the hospital because my son had been stabbed. When I arrived there, the doctor told me that he had a narrow escape from death. He was stabbed by Tootsie; yet despite it all, he loved her and his daughter very much. My son stayed with Tootsie for a while after that, but eventually, the relationship ended. He knew he could never have her back again.

From that point forward, his focus in life was just getting high every day. He stood at the corner with the other guys doing nothing but drinking and drugging. One day, I was over at a girlfriend's house, and his ex-girlfriend came there to tell me that my son had been shot in his buttocks by her boyfriend while his back was turned. When I went to the hospital, the doctors told me that they had to give him a reversible colostomy bag and that he would need someone to pack and unpack his wound; so, they showed me how to do it. It turns out that he had been shot with a double-barrel shotgun at close range. I thank God for his grace!

I brought him home and proceeded to nurse him back to health. He did not have any health insurance, so I purchased all his supplies—gauze, bags, etc. I unpacked and freshly packed his wound for about eleven months. He changed his own bag, which was a big help. Once his wound was about the size of a quarter, I no longer had to pack it. A couple of months later, he had an operation to reverse the colostomy bag, but things got worse for my son at that point.

He acted as if life was no longer worth living; he had no hope. He called me one night from a pay phone. He sounded like he wanted help but did not know how to ask for it. I tried my best to give him guidance. We talked for about an hour or more. I felt so bad, and I did not know what else to do or say. I did not know that my son was aware that when he came into this world, he was a product of rape. James was a kind person with a heart of gold. When he became an adult, we used to go to clubs together and just have fun.

One night, we were sitting on my porch, and I was a little depressed. He said, "Mom, look up at that star. That could be your mother!" I slowly look up; and there, up in the sky, was the brightest, biggest star blinking at that moment. I knew then that James believed in God. I had to say, "Thank you, Jesus." My son was out there. He became homeless, a drug addict, and started looking like a bum. I would give him money but eventually stopped; instead, I started buying him canned meats, bus tickets, etc.

One day, I saw my son standing on the corner with his toes sticking out of his shoes. This was during the winter. I ended up buying him some Timberland boots when I saw him again. The next time that I saw him, he did not have them on. Apparently, he sold them to someone. I brought him a coat, and he said someone had stolen it. I tried talking to him about different drug programs. I tried to have a green warrant taken out on him, which means you could have someone committed if they appear to be a danger to themselves. That did not work. There was nothing that I could do but pray.

My son would stay with me from time to time, but he would eventually go back to the streets. There was this one time when he had gotten beaten up badly at this club. Another time, his throat was cut. He had to have clamps to hold it together. My son would always stay with me until he got better, but he would still return to the streets. When he would stay with me, he would sleep in my king-size bed beside me. I guess I felt I almost lost him, and I wanted him to be close to me so that I could take care of him and protect him from any further harm.

After he recovered from that, I told him that God had given him warnings to straighten up his life. He got shot, stabbed, and had his throat cut. I begged him to get himself together because we love him, God loves him, I love him. I did not want to bury him; it is not supposed to be that way. He was supposed to bury me. I gave him the cross that was around my neck and put it around his.

A week or two later, he came over. I had both of my granddaughters with me then. He and I got into an argument. He always thought I loved the oldest granddaughter more than I did the younger one by Tootsie, but that was not true. I was never around the youngest granddaughter when she was younger because they lived two hours away. Yet I still loved them both the same.

Before he left, he said to me, "The next time I see you, you will be in your coffin, or I will be in mine." Then he left. Oh, how true those words became! Weeks went by, and I did not hear from him. I was going around the neighborhood, checking on him, trying to find out how he was doing through his friends. All seemed to be well, as far as I knew.

Shortly thereafter, I went out for my birthday. When I returned home, my daughter told me that my son had stopped by with a female friend and brought me a birthday card. I was so happy to hear that he looked well and clean and had a friend. I felt as if things were going well for him, and I was very pleased.

About two weeks after my birthday, as I was coming home, I got off the bus and headed toward my house. As I got closer to my home, I saw that Tootsie and her daughter-in-law were standing on my porch. I knew something awful had happened. I braced myself as I reached them. She said, "Dottie, James is in the hospital. You must come now."

They drove me to the hospital, and we went up to the hospice ward intensive care unit. I will never forget seeing my only son lying there. My firstborn, the one I grew up with, the one I could talk to about anything…We were friends—best friends. He was lying on the bed with tubes running from his head, draining the fluids out. His eyes were a little open, and his chest was moving.

They said that he was dragged by a car. The car window had been rolled up with his arms in it, and the driver sped off with my son hanging on. Then whoever held my son's arms through the window let go. His body went up in the air; and when he came back down, his head hit the ground. James suffered a massive head trauma.

I kissed him and rubbed my hands on him. The priest and the doctor came into the room. The doctor explained to me that my only son was brain dead and that the machines were the only things keeping him alive. He was on a ventilator that kept his heart pumping. They said that without the machines, nothing would happen.

They told me that there was nothing else they could do, and that they would have to unplug the machines because he had already been on them for three days. Due to them having a problem finding me, his next of kin, he had been labeled a John Doe. James had no identification on him when he was admitted to the hospital.

Tootsie asked the doctor if she could go get his daughters so they could see him before they disconnected the machines. She could only get in touch with her daughter. We all said goodbye to him, and then I said the words that no mother should ever have to say: "Go ahead, unplug the machine."

I walked out into the hallway while they all stayed until the end. I cried so hard and called to God, "Please help me!" My world fell apart that day. I never imagined that I would have to feel the pain I felt. As I am typing this chapter, tears are flowing down my cheeks. It is still hard for me, but I know that the Lord has him and that he is in a better place—no more pain, no more suffering. He is free now, and I truly know this from my heart. My son is in Heaven with the Lord.

I had life insurance on my son for a while, but it got to a point where I could no longer afford it. I canceled the policy a couple of months before he died. I did not have any money, and only God knew how I would be able to bury my son.

I continued to pray within myself to keep my mind intact and remain determined to let the Lord handle it. I then went to social services to get help. My longtime friend Betty and I went to churches to ask for help to bury my son. My God worked it out. James was able to have a chapel funeral with two pastors present. One of the pastors, I did not know his reason for being there until he spoke. He said that he was there because he knew my son James. He said that James had personally given himself to the Lord and that he was attending Bible classes every Wednesday.

Just hearing those words was a great comfort to me. There are no words that can explain how I felt in my heart. I was so overjoyed to know that after the storm, there was a rainbow. Thank you, Lord! Thank you. The people who were there did not understand what I meant as I kept saying it repeatedly as I rocked, but the Lord and I knew. Amen!

I cannot close this chapter in my life without speaking about the devil because he is a liar! My grandchildren and their mothers were at the chapel, and there was a disagreement that occurred that almost led to a fight. I quickly stepped in and reminded them all, "It is my son's funeral. Although he had lost his respect out there in the streets, he shall have it now." There was nothing more that needed to be said as we rode in the limo to Evergreen, his burial site. The pastor said a prayer and let the white doves fly up in the air. Oh, what a beautiful sight it was!

It took four years after his death for me to really stop grieving. I knew he was okay when one day as I was sitting on my sofa in the living room, crying and thinking about him. I had my mom's and my son's picture sitting on each side of the table.

Someone knocked at the door. I went to answer it, then when I turned back around, I saw my mom's picture facing my son's. I knew at that moment my mom was telling me that my son is fine and that he is with her. I stopped crying. Until this day, I think about him all the time. I think of the good times we shared together as mother and son, and I know that he is in Heaven with our Father. Amen.

My daughter Niva also told me about a dream she had. She said there was a knock on the door, and she answered it. There stood James dressed in all white, smelling good. A bright light was beaming behind him. She said he hugged her and told her he loved her. She realized that he had passed on, so she started pulling away from him. I guess he was trying to tell her not to be afraid. When she told me about the dream, I felt it was another sign that he was with God. If God gave his only Son, then surely, I could accept the fact that my son is gone. I love him dearly, but God loves him more.

Chapter 10

My Restoration

How I Became a Born Again Christian

. . . .

Prayer has been the key for me in everything. After the storms I have gone through, I have looked back at my life, and I have seen how many times the devil has tried to set me on fire. But God said, "No, she's mine." God showed me time and time again that He is real—He is real for you and for me. I have been clean from drugs and alcohol for over twenty years. I thank God!

I know that I am human and that I make mistakes; but because of God, I am making it, one day at a time. My Father knows my soul. I am doing my best to live a clean life. I have an appointment sometime later in life, it is an appointment that we all will have. That is when we must stand before God. All God wants us to do is to be real with Him.

Once God has forgiven you, something amazing happens. It is such an awesome part of this process. God brings restoration to us. I give the Almighty God all the praise and all the glory because

He is a mighty God. He is an awesome God. He is a merciful God.

I had not been to church in many years. One Sunday morning, the Lord woke me up and told me that I was going to church. I took a shower and got a dress out of the closet. My daughter Niva asked me, "Where are you going?" I told her that I was going to church. She was surprised.

I went out the door and started walking up the street. I passed two churches and went across the street. The Lord led me to this small building. The building looked like it used to be a garage. I went in and sat in the last row, and the pastor asked me if I was the woman who called. I told him no, and he said it was okay. "You are welcome," the pastor said. I stayed for the service and was a member for five years or so, up until I moved out of the state.

It was the Lord who woke me up that morning and said, "You are going to get saved from your past." I love the Lord with all my heart and soul. I am not perfect—in fact, no one is. Yet Jesus has forgiven me more than I can imagine. He has saved my life. He has given me so much. He brings me joy. I do not worry anymore. I do not feel hatred for anyone. My God has given me a new outlook on life, and I am blessed with God's grace. I am a living witness that there is a God, and He is a mighty awesome God.

I am so glad that I found Him…or shall I say He found me. God can find you too. There is nothing too great or too small that our Father can't handle. But you must let go, give all your burdens to Him. Believe in the Lord, Jesus Christ with all your heart. Believe in His death, burial, and resurrection. repent, ask for forgiveness and you will be saved! God wants you; He loves you. God is a forgiving God. He does not make mistakes. He's perfect in every way.

I thank you, Lord, and O how I praise your name! Without you, I would not have been here. Lord, I thank you. I thank you. Hallelujah!

My brother Jimmy was locked up for thirty-seven years, and now he's a free man! Amen! Thank you, Lord! Jimmy has grown sons whom I love dearly.

From the Author

· ·

This is my true-life story. I did not cut any corners. I told the good and the bad. Names have been changed to protect privacy. I pray that my life story will help people all over the world. Miracles happen every day. I am living proof; I do believe in miracles.

I want you to know, I love you. God, our Father loves you and only wants your love in return. You are not alone.

The roads of my life have not been easy but with the Lord, on my side, there is no such thing as impossible. Whatever I do, whatever I went through, or whatever I will go through I will never lose my faith. Psalm 121:1 I lift up my eyes unto the hills where does my help come from? My help comes from the Lord, the Maker of Heaven and Earth.

Whatever happens in life, never lose your faith. Jesus is there for you and with you. Stand on His promises and read your bible. He will never leave nor forsake you. Never doubt Him. Sometimes the roads in our lives may seem unbearable but He is there. He is God, a forgiving, passionate, and faithful God! Miracles do happen.

About the Author

· ·

Praise God! I was born on October 5, 1954, at 6:28 a.m. My father named me after his mom, Diza, which is a Hebrew name that means joy. I pray this story will bring you joy in knowing that you are not alone. Our Father in Heaven is there with us through the good and the bad times. He loves all of us. I never finished the eighth grade, but I thank God I had common sense.

While I was locked up, I began writing notes in my little diary, not knowing that the things I was documenting would be my Story, my Testimony, for my book. I realized everything I had been through was a part of God's plan for my life. May our Father bless and forever keep you. Hallelujah, Jesus!

I was depressed one day and started crying, and these are the words I sang out to my Father, that I want to share with you.

> I talked to my Father, and all of my tears went away.
> I talked to my Father because it's a new day.
> My Father said, "Wipe your tears. Don't weep no more.
> It's a new day. I gave you your life because I heard you.
> Don't cry no more.
> I am your Father, and you are my child.
> I will take care of you. I love you.
> Your Father." (author unknown)

In loving memory of Diza Sutton

May 04, 2021

Printed by Libri Plureos GmbH in Hamburg,
Germany